Disney
THE BFG

MUSIC FROM THE ORIGINAL MOTION PICTURE SOUNDTRACK

MUSIC COMPOSED AND CONDUCTED BY JOHN WILLIAMS

ISBN 978-1-4950-7173-7

T0056116

HAL•LEONARD®

7777 W. BLUEMOUND RD. P.O. BOX 13819 MILWAUKEE, WI 53213

Visit Hal Leonard Online at www.halleonard.com

OVERTURE

By JOHN WILLIAMS

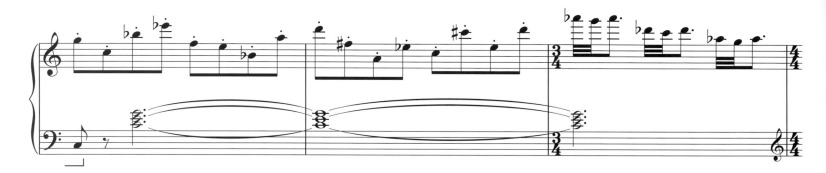

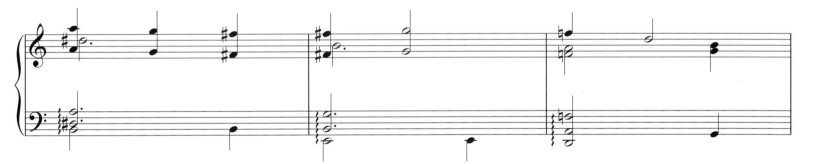

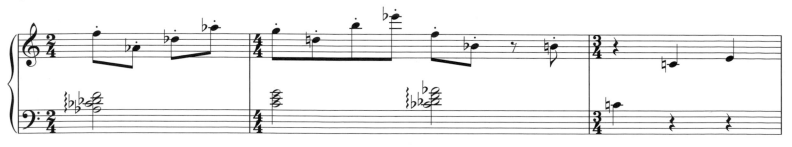

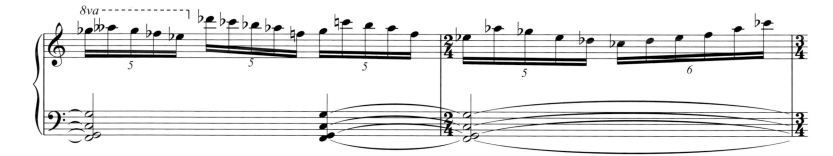

TO GIANT COUNTRY

By JOHN WILLIAMS

Moderate Waltz

Moderately

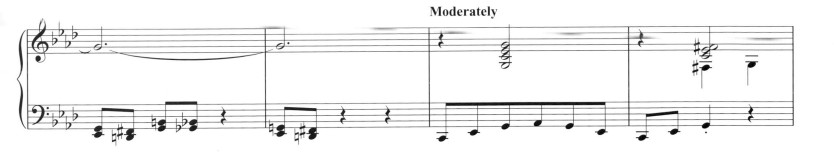

BUILDING TRUST

By JOHN WILLIAMS

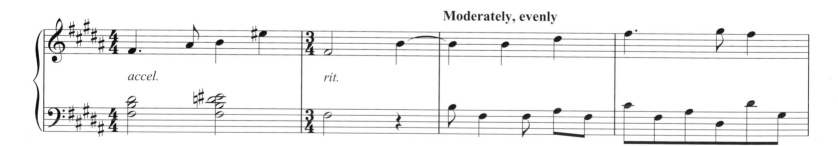

Slightly slower, freely

Moderately, steadily, in 2

Moderately slow, expressively

FROLIC

By JOHN WILLIAMS

Fast March

BLOWING DREAMS

By JOHN WILLIAMS

Moderately, expressively

Slightly faster

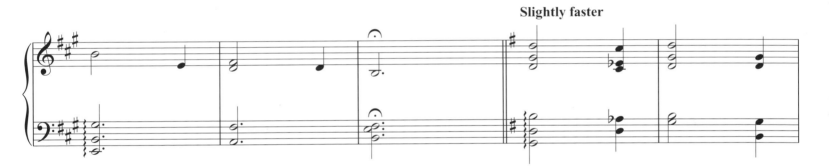

Slower, freely

Slightly faster, evenly

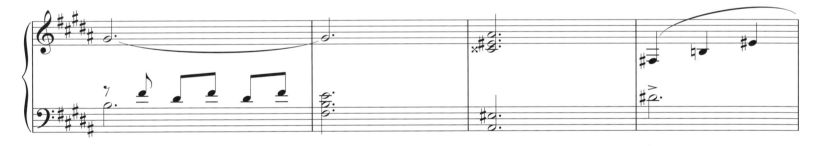
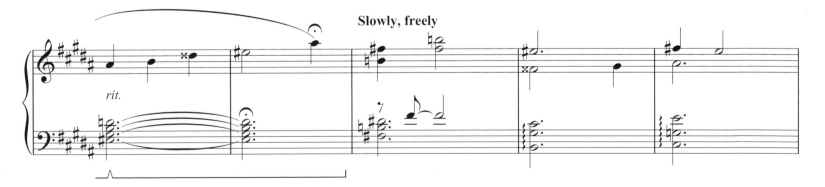
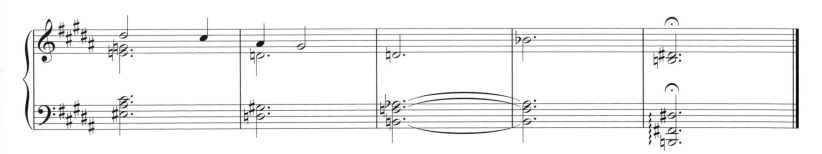

Slowly, freely

rit.

SNORTING AND SNIFFING

By JOHN WILLIAMS

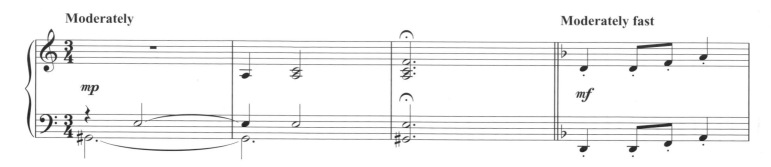

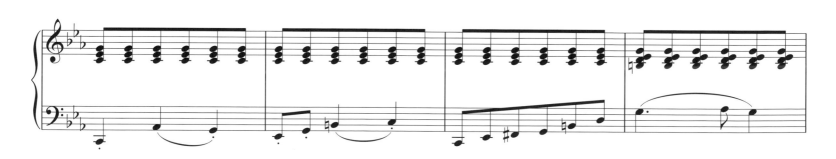

THERE WAS A BOY

By JOHN WILLIAMS

Moderately slow, expressively

mp

Pedal ad lib. throughout

SOPHIE'S THEME

By JOHN WILLIAMS

With innocence

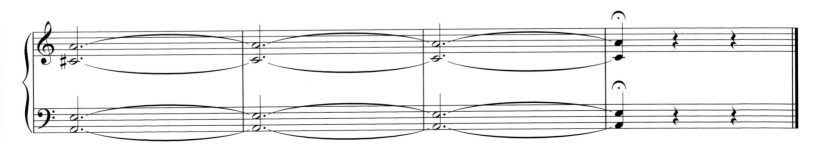

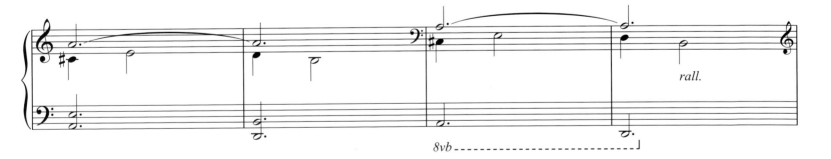

SOPHIE'S FUTURE

By JOHN WILLIAMS

Moderately slow, expressively

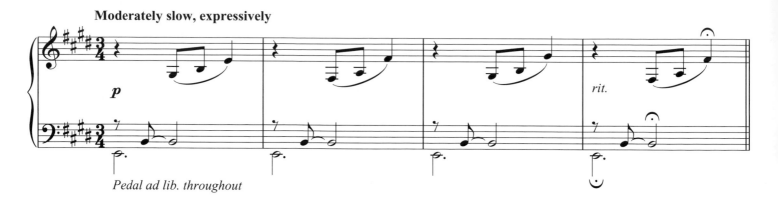

Pedal ad lib. throughout

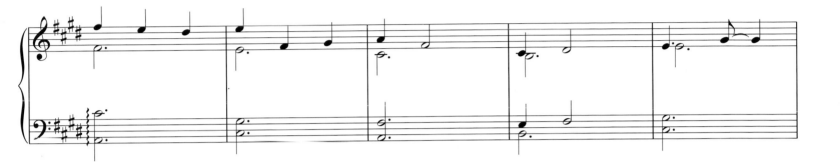

Moderately fast

Broadly

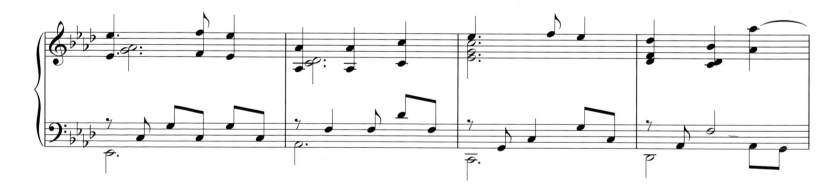

rit.